Cool Kids Cook

For Donna's nieces (who we love to pieces) Elisha + Gabrielle, Ness + Simon's beautiful new baby and Dan's wild child, Duke. Thanks and love to our big kids, too—Bill, Simon and John—for letting us play together on the weekends, and to our publisher, Catie Ziller, for leaving us to our own devices on this one, and trusting in the result.

Recipes: Donna Hay

Editor: Jane Price

Project Manager: Anna Waddington

Recipe Testing: Ben Masters, Briget Palmer

Art Director: Vanessa Holden

Illustrator: Danielle Holden

Designer: Anderson C S Mendes

HarperCollins books may be purchased for educational, business, or sales promotional use. For information please write: Special Markets Department, HarperCollins Publishers Inc., 10 East 53rd Street, New York, NY 10022.

Originally published in Australia in 2000 by Murdoch Books®, a division of Murdoch Magazines Pty Ltd.

FIRST U.S. EDITION PUBLISHED 2004

Library of Congress Cataloging-in-Publication Data has been applied for.

ISBN 0-06-056633-7

04 05 06 07 08 / 10 9 8 7 6 5 4 3 2 1

Cool Kids Cook

Donna Hay

with illustrations by Danielle Holden

WILLIAM MORROW
An Imprint of HarperCollins*Publishers*

inside

get cooking...

Cooking is cool. It's fun to do with your friends and family, and it's fun to share the food you make as well. The recipes in this book show how easy it can be. Each recipe leads you step-by-step to a new taste sensation. Make it easy on yourself by taking the time to read the safety, tips and tools pages up the front: they are full of good ideas. Also, check the ingredients and tools lists at the beginning of each recipe to make sure you're absolutely ready to go. Sometimes you may have to ask a grown-up for help, but that's OK (they do come in handy every so often). People love to get together over food—enjoy sharing what you make and get ready for all the compliments!

Safety

The levels of difficulty vary from recipe to recipe. Parents are requested to supervise their children in the kitchen at all times.

Ovens & Stovetops

- Ovens and stovetops are serious stuff—they get very hot and can give you a very very nasty burn. Ask an older person to help you, so that you can sail through your recipe. Treat your oven like the school-yard bully—be careful.

- Always use oven mitts when taking things in and out of the oven—the door, sides and racks are hot as the oven is preheated.
- Use oven mitts that are small enough for your hands—large oven mitts may get in your way and make it harder to handle hot baking trays.
- Arrange the racks in the oven before you turn on the oven to preheat it.

- If you use a wet dishtowel to remove hot baking dishes from the oven, the heat will go straight through the dishtowel and give you a nasty burn.
- It is best to put boiling pans at the back of the stovetop and never leave them unattended. Remember to turn off the oven or stovetop when you are finished.
- When you are plugging in your electric mixer, make sure your hands are dry. Check that the mixer is switched off at the dial before you turn on the power at the wall.

- Use a wire rack when cooling hot baking dishes so that you don't make scorch marks on the countertop.

● When cooking with a saucepan or frying pan, turn the handle to the side of the stovetop so that nobody can knock it and tip the hot contents over themselves or you. Be sure you don't turn the handle towards another element that is on or the handle will heat up and give you a bad burn when you try to pick up the pan.

● When opening the oven door, stand back so that the hot steam can escape before you remove your hot baking tray. Always wear your oven mitts and be sure that your path is clear before removing something from the oven to the counter.

● Wear an apron to protect your clothes and skin from any cooking splatters. Keep it tied around you, especially when you are working at the stove or oven.

Knives & Chopping

● If you are not experienced or big enough, ask an older person to do all the chopping required for the recipe. That way you'll avoid accidents with the knife.

● If you are chopping with a knife, always use a chopping board and be sure that the chopping board doesn't slip on the counter. If it does slip, put a damp dishtowel underneath to keep it steady. Always wash the board and knife regularly between chopping raw meat products and fresh foods like vegetables or herbs.

● Remember not to put knives in the sink, especially when it is filled with water and suds. Somebody could reach in and give themselves a painful cut.

● Never cook in bare feet or open-toed shoes as a knife could drop or something hot could easily spill on your feet.

● When chopping something round like an onion or tomato, cut it in half first then put the cut side down on the chopping board so that you have a flat surface to cut on. It's easier and safer.

● If you are not confident chopping with a knife, roughly grate a peeled onion or carrot instead of chopping it.

and last but not least...

● If you spill something, clean it up before you slip in it—oops!

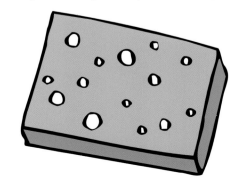

Tips

Getting things organized makes cooking a lot easier— here are some time-saving ideas

● Read the recipe all the way through before you start so that you are sure you have all the ingredients and tools. Set out the ingredients on the work surface so that they are within reach when you need them. Have them weighed out and prepared before you start.

● Preheat the oven before you start to cook so that it will have reached the right temperature by the time you are ready to use it.

● Clean up as you go along, otherwise you'll have a big pile of dishes to wash at the end. It is also safer to keep things tidy and out of your way.

● Measure liquids in a special jug and dry ingredients, such as flour and cocoa powder, in measuring cups.

● When you are measuring, make sure you fill to the top of the line you are measuring to— not under or over. When using cups to measure dry ingredients, smooth the top of the contents with a knife to make them level for an accurate measure.

● Sift dry ingredients, such as flour and cocoa powder, to remove any lumps before you add them to mixing bowls.

● When you are cooking, set a timer. When the buzzer goes off you know that your cooking time has finished.

● Spills should be cleaned up as soon as they are made. Spills on the floor are slippery, so wipe them up with paper towels. On the work surface, use a sponge.

● Wash fruit and vegetables before you cook them. Mushrooms just need a wipe with a damp piece of paper towel. Don't rinse them or they'll go soggy.

● Refrigerate fresh meat or chicken in a bowl loosely covered with plastic wrap. It will keep for 3 days like this.

● Before icing a cake or cupcakes, make sure that the cake is cold. If it is warm, the icing or cream will run straight off.

● Some ingredients in recipes are "optional". This means if you don't like something (like chili sauce) you can make the recipe anyway.

Tools

Choosing the right tool for the job saves time and energy. Here's a quick rundown on some of the tools you'll be using.

Measuring jugs

Are for measuring liquids like stock, milk and cream. Bend down and have your eyes level with the line on the jug for an exact measure. Measure level to the top of the line—not under or over. A good measurer is a good cook.

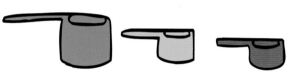

Measuring cups

Come in 1-cup (250 mL), 1/2-cup (125 mL), 1/3-cup (80 mL) and 1/4-cup (60 mL) measures. The cups are for measuring solids like rice, flour, cocoa powder, cookie crumbs and sugar. To measure properly, heap the ingredient up over the top of the cup. Then use a knife or spatula to sweep over the top and make it level. This is important when baking cakes and cookies.

Measuring spoons

Come in 1 tablespoon (15 mL), 1 teaspoon (5 mL), 1/2 teaspoon (2.5 mL) and 1/4 teaspoon (1.2 mL) measures. They are for measuring small amounts, like milk, baking powder and honey. Heap dry ingredients over the top, then use a knife or spatula to sweep over the top, making it level for an exact measure.

Kitchen scales

Are handy for weighing ingredients that are hard to measure accurately in cups—like chopped chocolate. The measure should be on zero to start, so put the bowl on first, then fill it with the ingredients.

Chopping board

Use a wooden or hard plastic board that is flat and clean. Always scrub clean when finished.

Knives

Are best kept sharp as less pressure is needed to cut. When you use less pressure, you are less likely to slip and cut yourself.

Saucepans

Have a set of saucepans in varying sizes. Small saucepans are good for melting butter or chocolate. Larger pans are great for boiling rice or pasta, or even making soup. They should have tight-fitting lids and solid handles that don't heat up when you are cooking in them.

Frying Pans

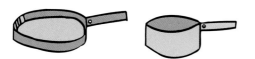

Are used to cook lots of foods. If you want to cook a stir-fry type of recipe like Chop Chop Suey

(page 46), then a deep frying pan with high sides is better so things don't splash over the sides. Non-stick frying pans are great because you can cook without oil and they are easy to clean. Always use one with a steady solid handle that doesn't heat up when you cook in it.

Wok

Is a deep round frying pan that is mainly used in Asian cooking. It is the perfect shape to toss all the ingredients around for a stir-fry. If you don't have a wok, you can use a deep frying pan instead.

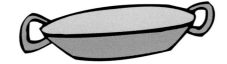

Stirring spoons

Can be either metal or wooden. When cooking curries, use a metal spoon as a wooden one will absorb the curry taste and may spoil your next cake mix.

Heatproof dish

Can be any dish that can stand the heat of the oven without cracking. If you are unsure, ask an older person or use a metal dish.

Baking trays and pans

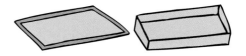

Are metal trays for cooking in the oven. The deep pans are for cooking things like Roast Chicken Dinner (page 53) and Gringo's Nachos (page 25), while the flat trays are for cookies.

Colander

A colander with wide holes is used to drain pasta and boiled vegetables like potatoes. When you are draining hot things, the safest way is to place the colander in the sink and pour the hot contents into it. Be very careful and watch out for the steam as it rises.

Tools

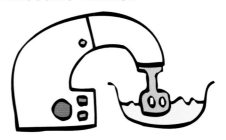

Can opener

Makes opening cans a breeze. Use a can opener that takes the top off inside the edge so that there is not a sharp exposed edge left behind. Always be careful to avoid nicks and cuts from the lid as the opener cuts through.

Grater

Is a kitchen essential for grating cheese and vegetables like carrots and potatoes.

Spatula

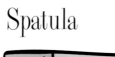

Is handy for turning things over in pans, or lifting them out. It's a large flat tool with a long handle so that you can pick up difficult things, such as fried eggs or pieces of pie.

Electric mixer

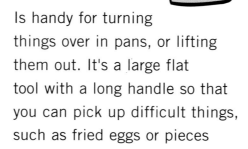

Makes cake-making easy. You may need the help of an older person to assemble the mixer and help you operate it. When making a cake, use the attachments that look like small whisks. If the mixer comes with a bowl, then use it. If it doesn't, then use a stable mixing bowl instead.

Mixing bowls

Use a bowl big enough to stir all the ingredients without them splashing over the sides. Metal or plastic bowls are great. Glass mixing bowls can be heavy—be careful not to drop them. A set of three mixing bowls is a good idea—small, medium and large.

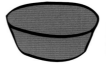

Sieve

A fine mesh sieve is used to sift dry ingredients like flour and cocoa to remove any lumps and ensure your cake mixture is airy and smooth.

Rubber Spatula

This is great for scraping bowls or spreading fillings or icings over cakes. Big wide spatulas are also good for lifting pieces of pie from baking dishes onto serving plates.

Cake tins

Come in lots of sizes and shapes—round, square and rectangular. You can write the sizes on the undersides of the tins so that you don't have to measure them every time.

Non-stick baking paper

Is available in the supermarket. It comes in a roll and is lightly coated in silicone so that cookies, cakes and any other cooked foods won't stick to the paper or the baking tray or tin. Using non-stick baking paper makes washing the dishes easy.

Skewers

Use a metal or wooden skewer to poke into the middle of a cake to see if it is cooked. If the skewer comes out clean, then the cake is cooked. If the skewer comes out with wet mixture on it, then the cake needs more cooking time.

Cookie cutters

Come in lots of different shapes—stars, circles and gingerbread men. These are great for making Spaceman Eggs (page 17) or Strawberry & Cream Stars (page 93).

Wire racks

Are for cooling cakes or cookies. It is best to cool cookies on wire racks so that they turn crisp and not soggy. Wire racks are also great for putting hot dishes and pans on so that you don't scorch the counter.

Pastry brush

Is a handy tool for brushing pastry with melted butter or milk before cooking so that the pastry top turns golden. A pastry brush is also useful for brushing marinade on steaks, kebabs and chicken. Wash it well after use and let it dry on a window sill before you put it away.

Simple conversions

1 cup butter = 250 g
1 cup flour = 125 g
1 cup rolled oats = 90 g
1 cup sugar = 220 g
1 cup icing (confectioner's)
    sugar = 155 g

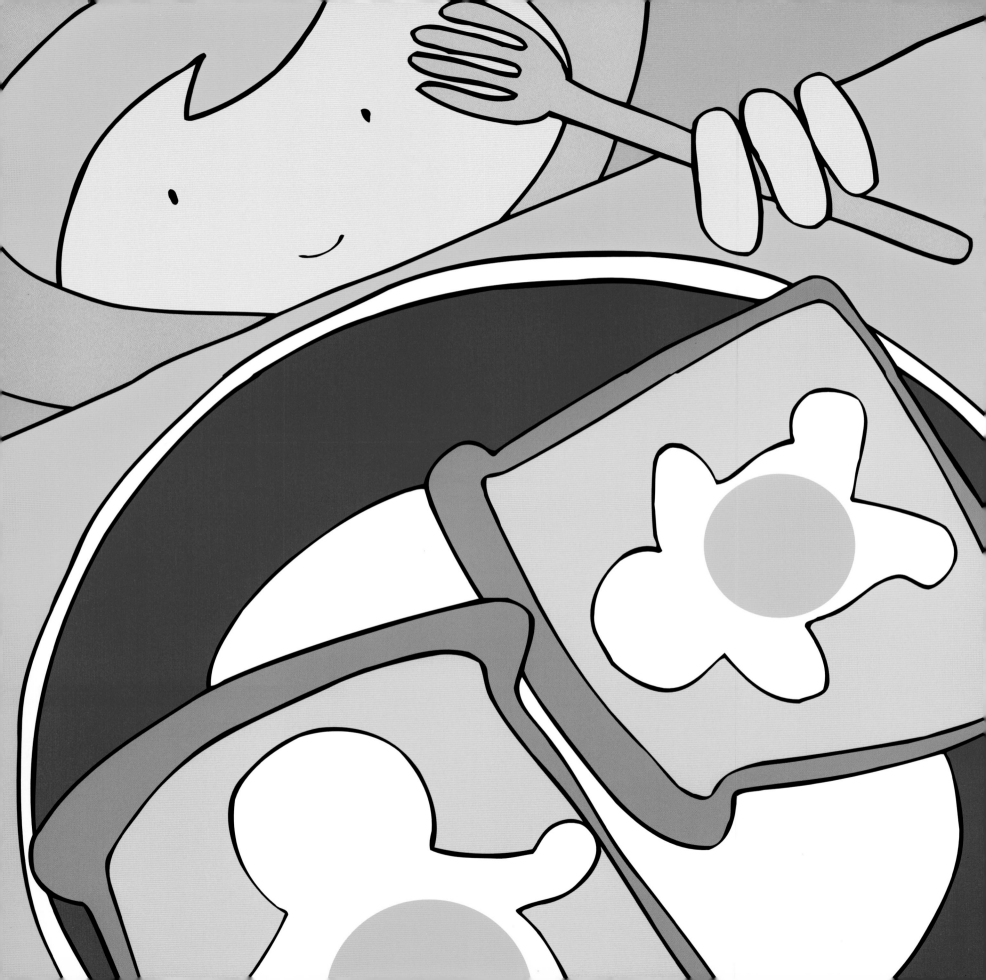

Spaceman Eggs

Yummy buttered toast blasts off into space with a runny, gooey, eggy center

ingredients

2 slices bread
1 tablespoon butter
2 small eggs

tools

gingerbread man cookie cutter
frying pan
spatula
cup

Use the cookie cutter to cut a man shape from the middle of each slice of bread. If you don't have a man-shaped cookie cutter, a star or round shape will do.

Heat the butter in a frying pan over medium heat and wait for it to melt. Place both slices of bread in the pan and cook until they are golden underneath. Turn the bread over with the spatula so that the golden side is on top.

Crack one of the eggs into a cup and then pour it into the man shape in one of the slices of bread. Do the same with the other egg and slice of bread. Cook for 4 minutes, or until the egg is cooked the way you like it. Serves 2

Jungle Curry

Feel the beat of the jungle in your mouth with this fiery (as you like) curry

ingredients

1 tablespoon oil
1 onion, chopped
2 teaspoons red curry paste
2 1/2 cups (625 mL) coconut milk
4 chicken breast fillets, sliced

1 red pepper, chopped
1 cup (60 g) chopped greens,
   such as beans or broccoli
rice or noodles, to serve

tools

knife + chopping board
measuring jug, cups + spoons
frying pan
stirring spoon

Heat the oil in a large frying pan over medium-high heat. Add the onion and cook, stirring, for 3 minutes, or until the onion is soft.

Add the curry paste and cook for 1 minute. Add the coconut milk to the pan and let it simmer for 5 minutes.

Add the chicken, pepper and greens and let the curry simmer for 5 minutes, or until the chicken is cooked. Serve with rice or noodles.
Serves 4

Tip For a milder curry add less curry paste—for more fire just add more

Chicken Noodle Soup

Oodles of noodles and yummy chicken will make this soup a family favorite

ingredients

6 cups (1.5 litres) chicken stock
3 chicken breast fillets, chopped
5 oz (140 g) instant noodles
salt and pepper
chopped parsley, optional

tools

measuring jug
knife + chopping board
saucepan
stirring spoon
ladle

Place the chicken stock in a saucepan over high heat and wait for it to boil.

Add the chicken and stir so that the pieces don't stick together. Let the chicken cook in the stock for 4 minutes.

Add the noodles to the saucepan with a little salt and pepper and cook for 3 minutes, or until the noodles are soft. Ladle into bowls and sprinkle with parsley, if you like.
Serves 4

Mountains O'Macaroni

When things turn chilly, warm up with mountains of creamy cheesy pasta

ingredients

1 1/2 cups (235 g) macaroni
1/2 cup (125 mL) cream
1/2 cup (60 g) grated
   cheddar cheese

tools

measuring jug + cups
grater
saucepan
colander
stirring spoon

Place a saucepan of water over medium-high heat and wait until it boils. Add the macaroni and cook for 8 minutes, or until the macaroni is soft.

Drain the macaroni in a colander and then put it back into the saucepan. Turn the heat to low and put the pan back on the heat.

Add the cream and cheese to the macaroni and stir until the cheese has melted and the mixture is thick.
Spoon into bowls to serve.
Serves 2

Gringo's Nachos

Round up your gringos to help make and share this spicy Mexican favorite

ingredients

6 1/2 oz (200 g) corn chips
2 cups (250 g) grated
   cheddar cheese
2 tomatoes, chopped
4 green onions, chopped
2 tablespoons mild chili sauce
12 oz (400 g) can red kidney
   beans, rinsed

tools

grater
measuring cups + spoons
knife + chopping board
can opener + sieve
deep baking tray + oven mitts
bowl
stirring spoon + spatula

Preheat the oven to 350°F (180°C). Place the corn chips in a deep baking tray and sprinkle with half the cheese.

In a bowl, mix together the tomatoes, onions, chili sauce and beans. Spoon the mixture over the corn chips, then sprinkle with the rest of the cheese.

Bake in the oven for 25 minutes. Scoop out the nachos and serve with guacamole (page 54), if you like.
Serves 4

Spaghetti Bolognese

Give your tastebuds a treat—take them to Italy for the night

ingredients

2 teaspoons oil
1 onion, chopped
1 lb (500 g) ground beef
14 fl oz (398 mL) tomato pasta
   sauce or canned tomato purée
13 oz (400 g) spaghetti

tools

measuring spoon
knife + chopping board
frying pan
stirring spoon
saucepan
colander

Heat the oil in a large frying pan over medium-high heat. Add the onion and cook for 4 minutes, or until the onion is soft. Add the beef and cook, stirring, for 5 minutes, or until the meat is brown.

Add the tomato sauce or purée and leave the sauce to simmer for 10 minutes, or until it has thickened.

While the bolognese sauce is simmering, cook the spaghetti in a large saucepan of boiling water for 10 minutes, or until it is soft. Drain the spaghetti in a colander and pile into serving bowls. Top with the bolognese sauce. Serves 4

Shepherds Pie

A double flavor whammy of meaty sauce and creamy potato packed into a pie

ingredients

- 1 recipe bolognese sauce (page 26)
- 4 large potatoes, peeled and chopped
- 1/3 cup (80 mL) milk
- 2 tablespoons butter
- 1 cup (125 g) grated cheddar cheese

tools

- vegetable peeler
- knife + chopping board
- measuring jug, cups + spoons
- grater
- heatproof dish
- saucepan
- colander
- bowl
- potato masher
- large spoon
- oven mitts

Make the bolognese sauce (without the spaghetti) and pour it into a heatproof dish. Preheat the oven to 350°F (180°C).

Cook the potatoes in a large saucepan of boiling water for 8 minutes, or until they are soft. Drain the potatoes in a colander and then place them in a bowl. Add the milk, butter and half the cheese and mash with a potato masher until smooth.

Pile the potato on top of the bolognese sauce and sprinkle with the rest of the cheese. Bake in the oven for 25 minutes, or until the cheese on top is brown. Serves 6

Tex Mex Tortillas

It'll all be OK at the corral when you serve up these cheesy bakes

ingredients

1 recipe bolognese sauce (page 26)
8 tortillas or flat breads
1 1/2 cups (185 g) grated
   cheddar cheese
chili sauce, optional

tools

grater
measuring cups
large spoon
baking tray
oven mitts

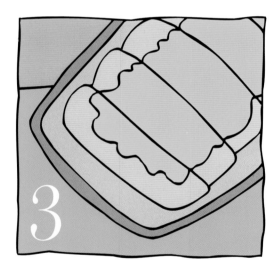

Make the bolognese sauce (without the spaghetti). Preheat the oven to 350°F (180°C).

Place the tortillas on a work surface and spoon bolognese sauce down the center of each one. Sprinkle with a little grated cheese and the chili sauce, if you like it.

Roll up the tortillas to enclose the filling and place them on a baking tray. Sprinkle the tortillas with the rest of the cheese and bake for 15 minutes, or until they are crispy.
Serves 4

Fried Rice

Confucius say "Fried rice is very nice, but sharing it is better"

ingredients

1 cup (200 g) white rice
1 1/2 cups (375 mL) water
1 tablespoon oil
3 green onions, chopped
2 slices ham, chopped
1 pepper, chopped

10 oz (300 g) can corn
 kernels, drained
3 tablespoons soy sauce
1 tablespoon sweet chili sauce

tools

measuring jug, cups + spoons
knife + chopping board
can opener
saucepan with lid
frying pan
stirring spoon

Place the rice and water in a saucepan over high heat and cook for 10 minutes, or until you can see tunnels in the rice and most of the water has been absorbed. Remove from the heat and put the lid on the pan. Leave for 5 minutes or until tender.

Heat the oil in a large frying pan over medium-high heat. Add the green onions, ham, pepper and corn and cook, stirring, for 4 minutes, or until the vegetables are soft.

Add the cooked rice, soy sauce and sweet chili sauce to the frying pan and stir so that the rice is mixed well and heated through.
Serves 4

Creamy Potato Salad

A favorite at BBQs and picnics—you'd better get to it before everyone else does

ingredients

1 ½ lb (750 g) baby new potatoes
4 slices bacon, rind removed
⅓ cup (90 g) mayonnaise
⅓ cup (90 g) sour cream
⅓ cup (20 g) chopped chives

tools

knife + chopping board
measuring cups
saucepan
fork
colander

bowl
stirring spoon

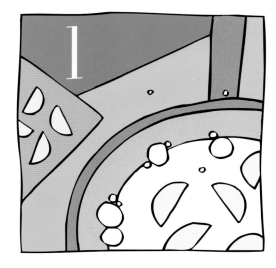

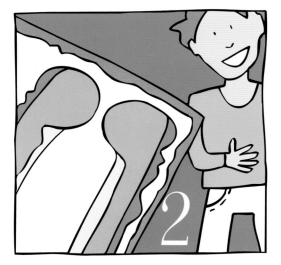

Cut the potatoes in half. Cook the potatoes in a large saucepan of boiling water for 7 minutes, or until they are soft when you poke them with a fork. Drain them in a colander and rinse under cold water to cool them.

Cook the bacon under a preheated broiler for 3 minutes each side, or until it is crisp. Let it cool, then break the bacon into small pieces.

Place the mayonnaise, sour cream and chives in a big bowl and mix them together. Add the potatoes and bacon and mix it all together before serving.
Serves 4–6

Garlic, Herb & Cheese Breads

Bread doesn't need to be boring—these are the perfect start to a meal

ingredients

4 long buns or small baguettes

garlic butter

2 cloves garlic, crushed

3 tablespoons butter, softened

herb butter

2 teaspoons mixed dried herbs

3 tablespoons butter, softened

cheesy butter

1/2 cup (60 g) grated cheddar
cheese

2 tablespoons butter, softened

tools

garlic press

3 bowls

measuring cups + spoons

grater

knife + chopping board

aluminum foil

baking tray + oven mitts

Preheat the oven to 350°F (180°C). Slice the bread all the way along, but without cutting all the way through it.

To make the different butters (or just one or two), place the garlic and butter, herbs and butter and cheese and butter in separate bowls and mix well. Spread the butter into the cuts in the bread.

Wrap the bread in aluminum foil and put on a baking tray. Bake in the oven for 15 minutes so that the butter melts and the bread is warm. Serves 4–6

Teriyaki Chicken

Yummy chicken, crunchy vegetables and slippery noodles—this recipe WOKS!

ingredients

2 teaspoons oil
1 onion, chopped
3 chicken breast fillets
1 teaspoon cornstarch
1/3 cup (80 mL) teriyaki sauce

2 carrots, peeled and chopped
1 green pepper, chopped
1 tablespoon brown sugar
rice or noodles, to serve
2 tablespoons sesame seeds

tools

measuring jug, cups + spoons
knife + chopping board
vegetable peeler
frying pan or wok
stirring spoon + bowl

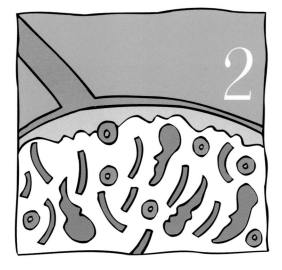

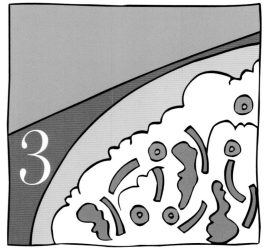

Heat the oil in a frying pan or wok over medium-high heat. Add the onion and stir for 3 minutes, or until it is soft. Slice each chicken fillet into pieces and add to the frying pan. Cook the chicken for 4 minutes, or until golden brown.

Put the cornstarch and teriyaki sauce in a bowl and mix together so there are no lumps. Add to the frying pan with the carrots, pepper and brown sugar. Cook for 5 minutes, or until the chicken is cooked.

Spoon into serving bowls with rice or noodles. Sprinkle with sesame seeds before serving. Serves 4

Hawaiian Pan Sandwich

Aloha! Treat yourself to a taste of the tropics with these lush sandwiches

ingredients

4 slices bread
butter
2 big slices ham
2 rings canned pineapple
2 big slices cheddar cheese

tools

can opener
butter knife
frying pan
spatula

Place a frying pan over medium heat and wait for it to warm up. While you're waiting, spread both sides of the bread with butter.

Pile 2 slices of the bread with ham, pineapple and cheese. Top with the other 2 slices of bread to make sandwiches.

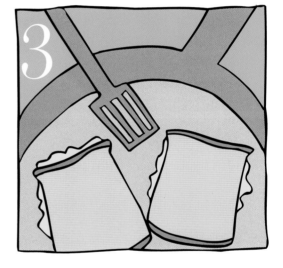

Place the sandwiches in the pan and cook for 2–3 minutes, or until golden brown and crispy underneath. Turn them over with a spatula and cook for another 2 minutes. Serve them while they are warm and toasty.
Makes 2 sandwiches

Honey & Peanut Lamb Kebabs

Eat these bit by bit off the skewers or by the forkful from a plate

ingredients

10 oz (300 g) lamb, cubed
1 green pepper, cubed
1 zucchini, thickly sliced
1 small container cherry
   tomatoes

3 tablespoons honey
2 tablespoons peanut butter
1 tablespoon soy sauce
salad, to serve

tools

knife + chopping board
measuring spoons
8 skewers
bowls
pastry brush

Carefully slide a cube of lamb onto a skewer, then a piece of pepper, zucchini and tomato. Add more pieces (in the same order) until the skewer is full. Do the same with the other skewers.

Mix together the honey, peanut butter and soy sauce and brush over the skewers.

Cook the skewers under a pre-heated broiler for 7 minutes or until the lamb is cooked. As they are cooking, brush them occasionally with the honey mixture. Serve with salad. Makes 8 skewers

Tip For wooden skewers, soak them in water for 20 minutes before you start, to stop them burning

Stuffed Baked Potatoes

Stuff your baked potatoes so they burst at the seams with tasty toppings

ingredients

4 large potatoes, scrubbed and
washed

oil, to brush

cheese and bacon filling

1 cup (125 g) grated cheddar cheese

1/2 cup (125 g) sour cream
or yogurt

2 slices bacon, cooked

cheese and avocado filling

1 cup (125 g) grated cheddar
cheese

1/2 cup (125 g) sour cream
or yogurt

1/2 avocado, chopped

tools

grater

measuring cups

knife + chopping board

baking tray

pastry brush

oven mitts

skewer

Preheat the oven to 400°F
(200°C). Place the potatoes on a
baking tray and brush them with
a little oil. Bake in the oven for
45 minutes, or until they are soft
when you poke them with a skewer.

Prepare the cooked potatoes for
the toppings by cutting a deep
cross in the top of each one.

Spoon the cheese, sour cream
and bacon or the cheese,
sour cream and avocado into
the potatoes. Or make up
your own topping using your
favorite ingredients.

Serves 4

Chop Chop Suey

Try a little kitchen kung-fu and whip up this quick Chinese takeout favorite

ingredients

2 slices rump steak
1 tablespoon oil
1 onion, chopped
1 pepper, chopped
1 carrot, peeled and chopped
2 sticks celery, chopped

6 1/2 oz (200 g) fresh hokkien
   or egg noodles
1 tablespoon cornstarch
3/4 cup (180 mL) pineapple juice
3 tablespoons honey
1/3 cup (80 mL) soy sauce

tools

vegetable peeler
measuring jug, cups + spoons
knife + chopping board
frying pan or wok
stirring spoon
bowl

Cut any bits of fat off the steak and then slice the steak. Heat the oil in a large frying pan or wok over medium-high heat. Add the onion and stir-fry for 2 minutes, or until soft. Add the steak and stir-fry for 2 minutes, or until brown.

Add the pepper, carrot, celery and noodles to the frying pan and stir-fry for 2 minutes.

Put the cornstarch and pineapple juice in a bowl and mix well so there are no lumps. Add the honey and soy and then pour it all into the frying pan. Stir-fry for 3 minutes, or until the sauce is thick. Serve in bowls.
Serves 4

Sausage Rolls

Get on a roll and make a batch of these party treats to share around

ingredients

10 oz (300 g) ground beef
1/4 cup (60 g) tomato paste
1 egg
1/4 cup (25 g) dry breadcrumbs
1 sheet ready-rolled puff pastry
milk, to brush
tomato sauce, to serve

tools

measuring cups
bowls
stirring spoon
knife + chopping board
baking tray
pastry brush
oven mitts

Preheat the oven to 400°F (200°C). Put the ground beef, tomato paste, egg and breadcrumbs into a bowl and mix them together. Divide the mixture into 2 piles.

Shape each pile into a sausage as long as the sheet of pastry. Cut the pastry sheet in half and place a sausage down the center of each piece. Roll the pastry over to cover the sausage. Cut each long sausage roll into thirds.

Place the rolls on a baking tray with the seams facing down, then brush the tops with a little milk. Bake for 20 minutes, or until the pastry is golden. Serve with tomato sauce.
Makes 6

Baked Ham & Egg Buns

These buns are a real handful of flavor

ingredients

2 round buns
2 eggs
1 slice ham, chopped
1/4 cup (30 g) grated cheddar
   cheese

tools

knife + chopping board
grater
measuring cups
bowl
fork

baking tray
oven mitts

Preheat the oven to 315°F (160°C). Slice the tops from the buns and dig out the fluffy bread inside so that the buns are hollow.

Put the eggs in a bowl and stir them with a fork. Place the ham and cheese inside the buns, then pour in the egg.

Place the buns on a baking tray and bake for 25 minutes, or until the filling is golden and set. You can eat the buns warm or cold.
Serves 2

Roast Chicken Dinner

Not just for Sundays, this is an every-day-of-the-week family favorite

ingredients

3 ¼ lb (1 x 1.6 kg) whole chicken
4 potatoes, peeled and halved
4 wedges squash
4 carrots, peeled
vegetable oil, to brush

tools

vegetable peeler
knife + chopping board
roasting pan
pastry brush
oven mitts

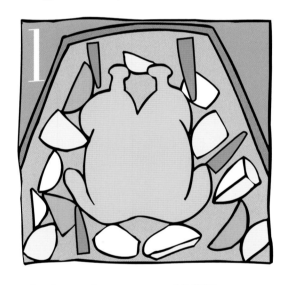

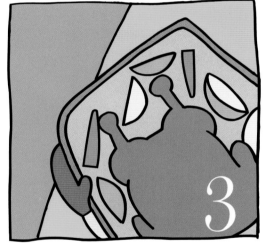

Preheat the oven to 400°F (200°C). Put the chicken in a roasting pan and place the potatoes, squash and carrots around it.

Use a pastry brush to lightly brush the chicken and vegetables with oil.

Bake for 1 hour, or until the vegetables are soft and the chicken is cooked through. Remove the chicken from the oven and carve it (you might need to ask an older person to help you). Serve with steamed green beans.
Serves 4–5

Tip To tell when the chicken is cooked, poke it with a skewer and the juices should be clear

Guacamole

Take a quick trip down Mexico way with this fiesta favorite

ingredients

1 avocado
1/2 cup (125 g) sour cream
2 tablespoons lime or lemon juice
cracked black pepper
chopped chives and chili sauce,
  optional

corn chips or Gringo's Nachos
  (page 25), to serve

tools

measuring cups + spoons
small sharp knife + chopping board
spoon and fork
bowl

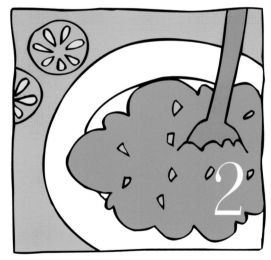

Cut the avocado in half with a sharp knife. Dig a spoon around the seed to lift it out. Spoon the avocado into a bowl and then mash it with a fork.

Add the sour cream, lime juice and pepper to the avocado and mix together.

If you like, sprinkle the guacamole with chives and chili sauce, then serve with corn chips or Gringo's Nachos.
Serves 4

Celebration Cake

You don't need a special occasion to party on with this perfect cake

ingredients

¼ cup (60 g) butter
1 cup (220 g) sugar
3 eggs
2 cups (180 g) dried coconut
1 cup (125 g) self-rising flour
⅓ cup (90 g) sour cream
1 cup (250 mL) whipped cream

icing

2 cups (310 g) icing
　(confectioner's) sugar
3 tablespoons butter, softened
3 tablespoons orange juice
3 tablespoons chocolate chips

tools

measuring jug, cups + spoons
electric mixer + bowl
stirring spoons
8 inch (20 cm) round cake tin
non-stick baking paper
skewer + oven mitts

Preheat the oven to 315°F (160°C). Place the butter and sugar in the bowl of an electric mixer and beat until light and creamy. Add the eggs, one at a time, and beat well. Fold in the coconut, flour and sour cream and mix well.

Line an 8 inch (20 cm) round cake tin with non-stick baking paper. Spoon the mixture into the tin and bake for 45 minutes, or until the cake is cooked in the middle when you poke a skewer into it. Leave the cake until it is completely cold.

For the icing, mix together the sugar, butter and orange juice in a bowl. Stir in the chocolate chips. Slice the cake in half and spread the bottom with cream. Put the top layer back on and spread with the icing. Serves 8–10

Oaty Scout Cookies

Scout's honor—these cookies will be a hit at your next fund-raising drive

ingredients

1 cup (100 g) rolled oats
1 cup (125 g) all-purpose flour
1/2 cup (110 g) sugar
3/4 cup (65 g) dried coconut
2 tablespoons golden syrup
1/2 cup (125 g) butter

1/2 teaspoon baking soda
1 tablespoon hot water

tools

measuring cups + spoons
bowls
saucepan
stirring spoons
2 baking trays + oven mitts
wire cooling racks

Preheat the oven to 315°F (160°C). Place the oats, flour, sugar and coconut in a large bowl.

Put the golden syrup and butter in a saucepan over low heat and let them melt. Mix the baking soda with the water and add to the pan. Pour the butter mixture over the dry ingredients in the bowl and mix together well.

Place flattened tablespoons of the mixture onto baking trays, leaving space between the cookies so they can spread. Bake for 8–10 minutes, or until golden. Cool on wire racks.
Makes 28

Chocolate Bombs

It's the explosive chocolate flavor that makes these muffins dynamite

ingredients

1 cup (250 g) butter
3 eggs
1 cup (220 g) sugar
1 teaspoon vanilla
2/3 cup (85 g) all-purpose flour
1/3 cup (40 g) cocoa powder

tools

measuring cups + spoons
saucepan
bowl
stirring spoon
sifter
oven mitts

twelve 1/2-cup (125 mL)
   non-stick muffin tins
skewer

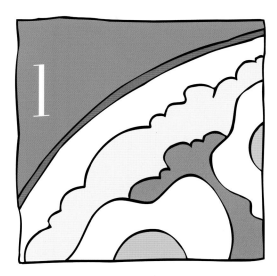

Preheat the oven to 350°F (180°C). Put the butter in a saucepan over low heat and leave to melt. Put the eggs, sugar and vanilla in a bowl and mix well.

Sift the flour and cocoa into the sugar mixture and then add the melted butter and mix well.

Pour the mixture into twelve 1/2-cup (125 mL) non-stick muffin tins and bake for 15 minutes, or until the muffins are cooked in the middle when you poke a skewer into them. Cool them in the tins.
Makes 12

Tangy Lemon Spread

This zesty spread is a perfect treat on freshly sliced bread or warm toast

ingredients

1/3 cup (90 g) butter
1 cup (220 g) sugar
1/2 cup (125 mL) lemon juice
2 eggs

tools

measuring jug + cups
heatproof bowl
saucepan
stirring spoon
screw-top jar

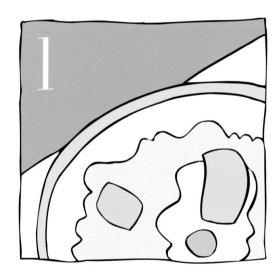

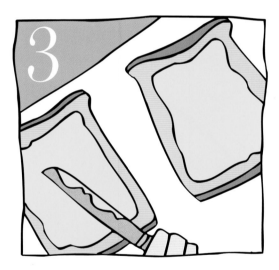

Place the butter, sugar, lemon juice and eggs in a heatproof bowl and place on top of a saucepan of simmering water.

Stir for 5 minutes, or until the mixture thickens, then remove it from the top of the saucepan—be careful of the steam.

Pour the lemon spread into a clean screw-top jar and keep it in the fridge. It can be spread on toast or sandwiches or over a cake. Makes 2 cups

Tip This spread can be kept in the fridge for up to 4 weeks

Thumbprint Cookies

Go undercover and get your friends' fingerprints on file in these crisp cookies

ingredients

2/3 cup (160 g) butter
1 cup (220 g) sugar
1 egg
1/2 cup (60 g) self-raising flour
1 1/4 cups (155 g) all-purpose flour
jam or chocolate chips,
  to decorate

tools

measuring cups + spoons
electric mixer + bowl
stirring spoon
baking tray
non-stick baking paper
oven mitts
wire cooling racks

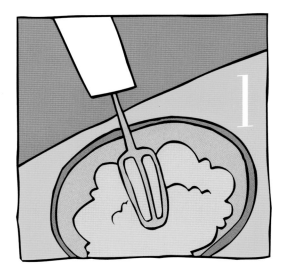

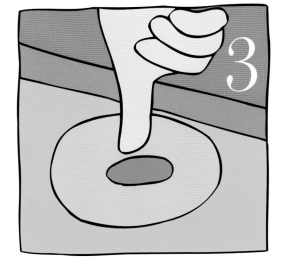

Preheat the oven to 350°F (180°C). Place the butter and sugar into the bowl of an electric mixer and beat until light and creamy. Add the egg and beat well. Stir in the flours and mix to a dough.

Line a baking tray with non-stick baking paper. Roll 2 tablespoons of the dough into a ball. Flatten onto the baking tray.

Press your thumb into the middle of the dough to make a hole. Fill the hole with jam or chocolate chips. Bake for 10–12 minutes, or until the cookies are golden. Cool on wire racks.
Makes 18

Chocolate Moon Rocks

Not quite space food, but definitely an intergalactic taste sensation—and easy!

ingredients

6 1/2 oz (200 g) dark baking
   chocolate, broken into pieces
1/3 cup (30 g) shredded coconut
1/2 cup (45 g) pink and white
   marshmallows, halved

tools

measuring cup
heatproof bowl
saucepan + stirring spoon
2 baking trays
non-stick baking paper

Put the chocolate in a heatproof bowl and place on top of a saucepan of simmering water. Stir until the chocolate is smooth, then remove it from the top of the saucepan—be careful of the steam.

Cool the chocolate slightly and then stir in the coconut and marshmallows. Line 2 baking trays with non-stick baking paper.

Pile spoonfuls of the mixture onto the trays so that they look like rocks. Place the trays in the refrigerator to let the rocks set. Makes 15

Ultimate Fudge Sauce

This chocolate sauce is so thick and delicious you'll want to take a dip in it

ingredients

6 1/2 oz (200 g) dark baking
   chocolate, broken into pieces
1 cup (250 mL) cream
ice cream, to serve

tools

measuring jug
saucepan
stirring spoon
bowl
screw-top jar

Put the chocolate and cream in a saucepan over low heat and stir until they make a smooth sauce.

Pour into a bowl and leave it to cool a little.

Pour the warm sauce over ice cream, or pour it into a clean screw-top jar and keep it in the fridge to use cold in a milkshake with lots of ice cream.
Makes 1 1/2 cups (375 mL).

Tip To reheat the sauce, place it in the microwave for a few seconds

Coconut Macaroons

Having an afternoon snack? Pile the plate high with these sweet chewy cookies

ingredients

2 egg whites
1/2 cup (125 g) sugar
2 cups (180 g) dried coconut

tools

measuring cups + spoons
2 baking trays
non-stick baking paper
bowl
stirring spoon
oven mitts

Preheat the oven to 350°F (180°C). Line 2 baking trays with non-stick baking paper.

Place the egg whites, sugar and coconut in a bowl and mix together. Press 2 tablespoons of mixture into a ball and put on the baking tray. Do the same with the rest of the mixture.

Bake for 8–10 minutes, or until the macaroons are just starting to brown. Cool on the trays before serving.
Makes 14

Buried Treasure Muffins

Follow this map, me-hearties, to discover the tasty hidden treasure

ingredients

2 cups (250 g) self-raising flour
1/2 teaspoon cinnamon
3/4 cup (185 g) sugar
10 oz (284 mL) sour cream
1 egg
3 tablespoons vegetable oil

3 bananas, roughly mashed
4 oz (125 g) milk chocolate,
   broken into chunks

tools

measuring cups + spoons
fork
bowls + stirring spoon
twelve 1/2-cup (125 mL)
   muffin tins
skewer + oven mitts

Preheat the oven to 400°F (200°C). Place the flour, cinnamon and sugar in a bowl and mix. Put the sour cream, egg, oil and bananas in a bowl and whisk together with a fork. Add to the dry ingredients and stir to just combine them.

Spoon the mixture into 12 greased 1/2-cup (125 mL) muffin tins until they are half-full. Place a chunk of chocolate on each one and then top with more muffin mixture.

Bake for 25–30 minutes, or until the muffins are golden and cooked in the middle when you poke a skewer into them.
Makes 12 muffins

Giant's Choc-Chip Mega-Cookies

You'll need a crane to crunch into these ginormous chunky choc cookies

ingredients

1/2 cup (125 g) butter, softened
and chopped
1/2 teaspoon vanilla
1 cup (230 g) brown sugar
1 egg
1 cup (125 g) all-purpose flour

1 cup (125 g) self-raising flour
1 cup (90 g) dried coconut
1 1/2 cups (225 g) chunks
of chocolate

tools

knife + chopping board
measuring cups + spoons
2 baking trays + oven mitts
non-stick baking paper
electric mixer + bowl
wooden spoon

Preheat the oven to 375°F (190°C). Line 2 baking trays with non-stick baking paper.

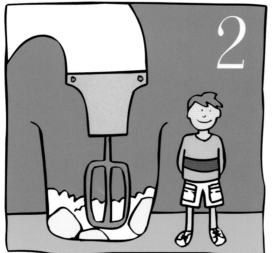

Put the butter, vanilla and sugar in the bowl of an electric mixer and beat until creamy. Add the egg and beat for 1 minute. Use a wooden spoon to stir in the flours, coconut and chocolate chunks.

Place a couple of big spoonfuls of mixture on each tray and bake for 20 minutes, or until the cookies are brown. Cool on the trays. The cookies are big so bake them in batches, a couple at a time.
Makes 10 giant cookies

Fairy's Cakes

Little cakes with little wings full of jammy, creamy things

ingredients

1 1/2 cups (185 g) self-raising
   flour
2/3 cup (160 g) sugar
1/2 cup (125 g) butter, chopped
3 eggs
1/4 cup (60 mL) milk
1 teaspoon vanilla
jam and whipped cream, to serve

tools

measuring jug, cups + spoons
knife + chopping board
electric mixer + bowl
two 12-hole cupcake tins
paper cupcake liners
oven mitts
teaspoon + stirring spoon

Preheat the oven to 350°F (180°C). Place the flour, sugar, butter, eggs, milk and vanilla in the bowl of an electric mixer and beat on medium speed for 4 minutes, until the cake mix is smooth.

Line two 12-hole cupcake tins with paper liners. Spoon the cake mix into the liners until they are three-quarters full. Bake for 18–20 minutes, or until the cakes have risen and are golden. Remove from the oven to cool.

Use a teaspoon to dig out a hole in the top of each cake. Save the small piece you've dug out and cut it in half. Fill the hole with jam and cream. Place the 2 small pieces on top of the cake to make wings.
Makes 24

Tutti-Frutti Jelly Cups

Wibble and wobble your way through these cups full of floating fruity chunks

ingredients

2 tablespoons gelatine powder
3 cups (750 mL) orange juice
1/2 cup (125 g) sugar
2 cups (400 g) chopped mixed
    fresh fruit or grapes and berries
ice cream, to serve

tools

measuring jug
cups + spoons
bowl
saucepan
stirring spoon
6 serving glasses or cups

Place the gelatine in a bowl and pour a little orange juice over the top to cover it. Leave for 5 minutes.

Put the sugar, the rest of the orange juice and the gelatine mixture into a saucepan over medium heat. Stir occasionally until the gelatine mixture is clear and has boiled.

Remove the pan from the heat and cool to room temperature. Place the fruit into 6 glasses and pour the cooled jelly over the top. Refrigerate for 1 hour, or until set. Serve topped with a scoop of ice cream, if you like.
Serves 6

Chocolate Fudge

Sink your teeth into these smooth chocolate chunks that we all love

ingredients

13 oz (400 g) dark or milk
chocolate, broken into pieces
1 cup (315 g) sweetened
condensed milk
1/4 cup (60 g) butter
colored sugar sprinkles

tools

measuring cup
saucepan
stirring spoon
8 inch (20 cm) square cake tin
aluminum foil
knife

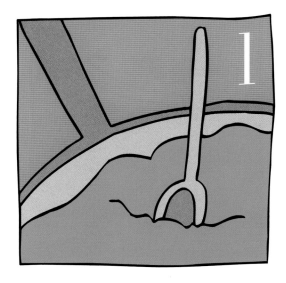
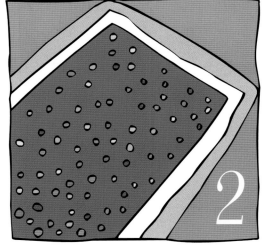
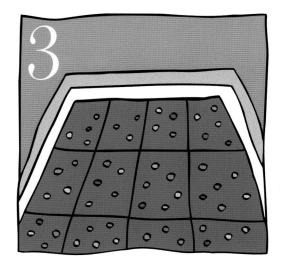

Put the chocolate, condensed milk and butter in a saucepan over low heat and stir until smooth and glossy.

Line an 8 inch (20 cm) square cake tin with aluminum foil and pour the mixture into the tin. Shake sugar sprinkles over the fudge and refrigerate for 2 hours, or until set.

Cut the fudge into small squares to serve or wrap pieces in waxed paper and twist the ends to make a great gift.
Makes 16 squares

Frog in a Pond

Fall hook, line and sinker for a fruity jelly hopping with frogs

ingredients

2 x 3 oz (85 g) packages green
   jelly mix
4 chocolate or gummy frogs

tools

4 serving glasses
jug

Make the jelly by following the instructions on the package. Divide the jelly in half and pour one half into a jug and set aside.

Pour the other half of the jelly into 4 wide glasses. Put the glasses in the freezer for 15 minutes, or until the jelly is beginning to set.

Place a chocolate or gummy frog on top of the jelly in each glass, then pour the other half of the jelly over the top. Refrigerate for 30 minutes, or until set.
Makes 4

Chocolate Mousse

Float away with deliciously squishy spoonfuls of this classic chocolate dessert

ingredients

6 1/2 oz (200 g) dark baking
  chocolate, broken into pieces
3 tablespoons butter
1/2 cup (125 mL) cream
4 egg whites
3 tablespoons sugar

tools

measuring cups + spoons
saucepan
stirring spoon
electric mixer + bowl
metal spoon
4 serving glasses

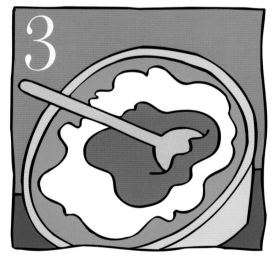

Place the chocolate, butter and cream in a saucepan over very low heat. Stir until the chocolate has melted, then take it off the heat and pour it into a large bowl to cool.

Put the egg whites in the bowl of an electric mixer and beat until light and foamy. Sprinkle with the sugar and beat until the egg white has peaks that stand up— be careful not to overbeat it.

Fold the egg white into the chocolate mixture with a metal spoon, being careful not to stir out the air. Spoon the mousse into glasses and refrigerate until firm. Serves 4

Bumpy Baked Custard

Sweet buried apricots make this dessert a bumpy but blissful ride

ingredients

1 tablespoon butter
14 oz (425 g) canned apricot
    halves, drained
2 tablespoons all-purpose flour
3 eggs
3/4 cup (180 mL) milk

3/4 cup (180 mL) cream
1/3 cup (75 g) sugar
1 teaspoon vanilla
ice cream, to serve

tools

can opener
measuring jug, cups + spoons
saucepan
4 cup (1-litre) heatproof dish
blender or food processor
oven mitts

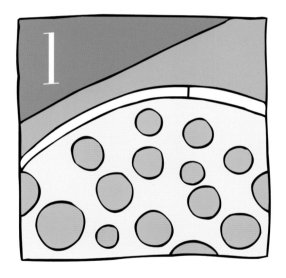

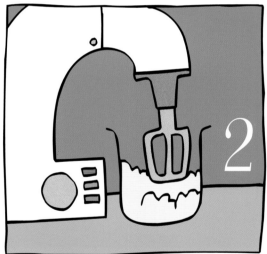

Preheat the oven to 315°F
(160°C). Put the butter in a
saucepan over low heat and leave
to melt. Place the apricot halves,
bump side up, in a greased
4 cup (1-litre) heatproof dish.

To make the custard, put the
flour, eggs, milk, cream, sugar,
vanilla and melted butter in a
blender or food processor and
blend until smooth.

Pour the custard over the apricots
and then bake for 30 minutes, or
until the custard is firm. Serve in
bowls with scoops of ice cream.
Serves 4–6

Marble Cake

Three favorite flavors swirl and twirl in one kaleidoscope of a cake

ingredients

1 cup (250 g) butter
1 cup (220 g) sugar
1 teaspoon vanilla
4 eggs
2 cups (250 g) self-raising flour
few drops red food coloring
3 tablespoons cocoa powder

tools

measuring cups + spoons
electric mixer + bowl
wooden spoon
3 bowls
8 inch (20 cm) round cake tin
skewer + oven mitts
wire cooling rack

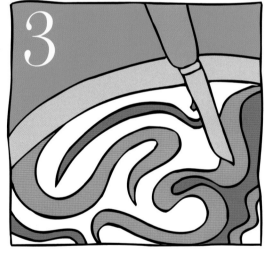

Preheat the oven to 315°F (160°C). Place the butter and sugar in the bowl of an electric mixer and beat until light and creamy. Add the vanilla and eggs, one at a time, and beat well. Use a wooden spoon to stir in the flour.

Divide the cake mix into 3 bowls. Mix a few drops of red coloring into one bowl and the cocoa powder into another. Leave one plain. Grease an 8 inch (20 cm) round cake tin and spoon all 3 mixtures into the cake tin.

Use a skewer or knife to swirl the mixtures together to create a marble effect. Bake for 40 minutes, or until the cake is cooked in the middle when you poke a skewer into it. Cool in the tin on a wire rack.
Makes 1 big cake

Crazy Cupcakes

Go crazy and color your cake any way you like it

ingredients

1 1/2 cups (185 g) self-raising flour
2/3 cup (140 g) sugar
1/2 cup (125 g) butter, softened
3 eggs
1/4 cup (60 mL) milk
few drops food coloring
   (any color)

icing

2 cups (310 g) icing
   (confectioner's) sugar
3 tablespoons soft butter
2 tablespoons hot water
food coloring (any color)
candies or sprinkles, to decorate

tools

measuring cups + spoons
two 12-hole cupcake tins
paper cupcake liners
electric mixer + bowl
spoon
oven mitts
sifter

Preheat the oven to 350°F (180°C). Line two 12-hole cupcake tins with paper liners. Put the flour, sugar, butter, eggs, milk and food coloring in the bowl of an electric mixer. Beat for 4 minutes, or until the cake mix is smooth.

Spoon the cake mixture into the paper liners until they are three-quarters full. Bake for 18–20 minutes, or until the cupcakes have risen. Remove from the oven to cool.

To make the icing, sift the icing sugar into a bowl and add the butter, hot water and a few drops of food coloring. Mix until smooth. Spread the icing over the cakes and top with candies or sprinkles. Makes 12

Strawberry & Cream Stars

Aim for the stars with these yummy jam and cream pastry sandwiches

ingredients

2 sheets ready-rolled puff pastry
1/3 cup (105 g) jam (any flavor)
1 cup (250 mL) whipped cream
icing (confectioner's) sugar,
   to dust

tools

measuring jug + cups
large star cookie cutter
baking tray
non-stick baking paper
oven mitts

knife
sifter

Preheat the oven to 350°F (180°C). Cut stars from the pastry, using a large star cookie cutter. Line a baking tray with non-stick baking paper.

Place the pastry stars on the baking tray. Prick the pastry stars all over with a fork. Bake for 8–10 minutes, or until the stars are puffed and golden. Leave to cool.

Slice the stars in half horizontally and spread the bottom halves with jam and cream. Put the tops back on and sandwich together. Dust with sugar before serving. Makes 14 stars

Chocolate No-Bake Squares

No need to get hot under the collar when whipping up these party favorites

ingredients

180 g (6 oz) shortbread cookies
filling
1 cup (250 g) butter
1 cup (250 g) cream cheese
1 cup (220 g) sugar

3/4 cup (90 g) cocoa powder
6 1/2 oz (200 g) shortbread
   cookies, broken into pieces

tools

measuring cups
9 inch (23 cm) square cake tin
aluminum foil
electric mixer + bowl
wooden spoon + knife

Line the base of a 9 inch (23 cm) square cake tin with aluminum foil. Arrange the cookies in rows to cover the base of the tin.

To make the filling, place the butter, cream cheese, sugar and cocoa into the bowl of an electric mixer and beat until smooth. Stir in the broken cookies with a wooden spoon.

Spread the filling over the cookie base and refrigerate for 2 hours, or until firm. Remove from the tin and cut into slices to serve. Makes 24 slices